BEATRIX POTTER,
SCIENTIST

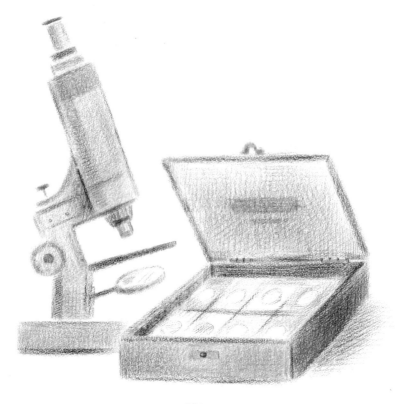

Lindsay H. Metcalf   *illustrated by* Junyi Wu

Albert Whitman & Company
Chicago, Illinois

For Will, who cheers me on
when I disappear into rabbit holes—LHM

To Jon, who's always been there
to dream big and explore with me—JW

Library of Congress Cataloging-in-Publication data is on file with the publisher.

Text copyright © 2020 by Lindsay H. Metcalf

Illustrations copyright © 2020 by Albert Whitman & Company ❋ Illustrations by Junyi Wu

First published in the United States of America in 2020 by Albert Whitman & Company

ISBN 978-0-8075-5175-2 (hardcover) ❋ ISBN 978-0-8075-5176-9 (ebook)

Printed in China

10 9 8 7 6 5 4 3 2 WKT 26 25 24 23 22 21

Design by Aphelandra Messer

For more information about Albert Whitman & Company, visit our website at www.albertwhitman.com.

You may know this girl, or who she'll become: someone who makes pictures of cuddly animals and writes your bedtime stories.

But there's more to *her* story.

She observes...

questions...

collects...

records.

Beatrix is a girl of science,
even if she may not know it yet.

See her there, giggling and splashing in the steps of the whistling postman?

His dirty boots carry him on mail routes past miles of mushrooms and moss. He can't help but look and learn from the lush landscape edging the Scottish Highlands.

Nature enchants Beatrix too. She absorbs
lessons on art and photography so she can
capture every rock, every flower,
every *thing*. This way, she can
take Scotland home.

Back on the outskirts of London, Beatrix sneaks nature inside, past her mother, past the staff. A bit older now, Beatrix and her brother Bertram fill their nursery with bunnies and bats and newts. Snakes and frogs and mice.

But when the animals die—
after she cries—she removes their
flesh to admire their bones.

There's care in every measurement,
from head to fingers to tail.
Beatrix draws them again and
again, outside and in.
That's science.

Now a young woman, Beatrix stows her specimens in London and sets off into the countryside with her family. She grabs her sketchbook and roams through northern England and Scotland, eyes open to the world so wide.

Always, she wants "to copy any beautiful object which strikes the eye."

Sometimes, she adds a twist of whimsy.

Always, she writes.

Look there—what does Beatrix see?

"Tiny fungus people singing and bobbing and dancing."

She blinks away the vision of fairies trotting among
the toadstools. But thousands of mushrooms remain.
"Joy of joys," she writes. They hold mystery on their own.

She peers closer and sees the colors.

She slices...

sketches...

and scopes...

every gill,

every scale,

every spore.

The microscope reveals a new world. Beatrix can't stop drawing. Who will understand? Probably not her parents. They have equipped her with cameras and experiences and tutors. But school is for Bertram.

Who will understand?

The Scottish postman! Of course!

The man she knew when she was little more than a spore herself. The shy postman who stashes plants in his satchel so he can study them at home.

Beatrix and Charles McIntosh discuss how to draw dainty details under the microscope. How to classify each fungus by name. They promise to share their work.

Beatrix's train returns to the city. Soon, a piece of Scotland arrives in London. Beatrix tears open the package from Charlie and inhales a mushroom's scent of fresh-cut hay. "Curiously strong & pleasant," she writes, and paints the samples with delicate strokes. Then she mails her artwork to Charlie.

Perhaps if Beatrix draws enough—
learns enough—her art could fill a science
book someday.

It's acceptable for Victorian women
like Beatrix to excel at painting.
Beatrix hopes to earn money, and
freedom from her parents' rule—
even if by selling silly pictures of
rabbits wearing coats.

Back in the country, Beatrix tugs up her starched dresses and trudges through the bogs, woodlands, and dung where mushrooms bloom.

She has questions:

How do fungi survive the winter? Do they spread underground? Is it true that spores sprout like seeds?

She wrecks her parents' London kitchen in her hunger for
answers. She concocts a solution to nudge the spores to life.
Toiling day and night in her ramshackle lab, Beatrix zooms
in with a microscope to check and record her specimens.
She can taste the breakthrough that is sure to come.

Finally, yes!

Spores *do* sprout like seeds, and Beatrix is among the first to grow them in Britain. Before long, the sprouts tangle in a network of filaments called mycelium. This must be the underground form Beatrix envisioned!

To be sure, she exhausts herself studying dense volumes on fungi, written in German. Then Beatrix drafts her findings for all of science to share.

A prominent natural history society could publish her paper. But it's the 1890s, and these London scientists do not allow women to join them.

Beatrix believes her work is too important to keep to herself. She earns a ticket to enter the Royal Botanic Gardens at Kew and mingles with some of Britain's best botanists. But most of the plant scientists there dismiss her as an amateur.

Beatrix may not be a professional, but she has pluck. She returns again and again, at first jumpy as a bunny, then growing braver, like a bull. She knows of a well-published scientist who can help—if she can convince him.

Her heart pounds. She clutches her slides and marches up to George Massee, one of the people in charge of Kew's plant specimens.

George has been trying to germinate spores with no luck. He peers through his spectacles with uncertainty.

George cannot deny that Beatrix has sprouted more than forty kinds of spores. He decides to try her methods.

Finally, success!

George agrees to present Beatrix's paper at a society meeting.

She waits for news. What is happening behind those doors?

George returns with a disappointing message about Beatrix's paper.

"They say it requires more work," she writes to her old friend Charlie.

So she withdraws her paper, rallies her resolve, and returns to her lab.

She sprouts more…observes more…draws more…

Until she doesn't.

What makes her stop? Does she suspect that she will never be taken seriously as a scientist? Does she begin to doubt herself?

Like pages ripped from a book, history holds those secrets.

But the next chapter is all there.

Beatrix Potter steps into the sunshine and tries
something else…something not altogether different.
　She pulls out an old letter, one with pictures.
A young friend had been sick in bed and needed
some good cheer.
　Her bunny, her Peter Rabbit, looks so real
on paper he nearly hops off the page.

This is no leap for Beatrix, even as she tucks away her fungi paintings for good.

She doesn't forget what she knows of nature. She follows her muse to a place where science informs art. A place of whimsy, grounded in fact.

Beatrix has studied every detail of her world—
small and big
flower and fungus
inside and out—
and molded it all into something new…

so she could share it with you,
and the whole world through.

MORE ABOUT BEATRIX POTTER

Born in 1866 to wealthy parents, Helen Beatrix Potter grew up observing everything around her. When her family left London and vacationed in the countryside, they carried sketchbooks. Beatrix wanted to know every little detail about her world, so she studied and drew a range of subjects—fossils, plants, insects, ancient artifacts—with scientific precision.

Some of Beatrix's earliest scientific endeavors revolved around the family's pets. Beatrix and Bertram kept a variety of animals: rabbits, yes, but also frogs, mice, birds, newts, a snake, and others. While the Potters adored their animals, they believed that after death, the animals' bodies were gifts for study. Many times, the children boiled them so they could remove the skin and muscles and preserve the skeletons. That may sound gruesome, but artists in the late nineteenth century often did this to understand how animals were built, so they could draw them accurately.

As a young girl, Beatrix traveled with her family each year to Scotland, where she met the postman naturalist Charles McIntosh. As an adult, she sought him out to show him her drawings of fungi. The shy, bewhiskered retiree with dirty boots became an unlikely mentor for a starched and pedigreed young woman like Beatrix. They shared common interests in the growth and classification of rare and common fungi, and he gave Beatrix tips about how to draw microscopic details. Beatrix continued to correspond with Charles throughout the 1890s and produced more than 350 drawings of fungi, mosses, and germinating spores.

Not only did Beatrix arrange for Charlie to send specimens of fungi, she spent more than ten years hunting for them herself. She found them in bogs, in the woods, on a broomstick outside her house—even on a piece of horse dung. She learned their scientific names and examined the specimens under a microscope, then drew them in various forms: whole, sliced, scraped, and sectioned.

She developed enough knowledge that she started seeking answers to questions about fungi that few professional scientists had asked. She took her results to the Royal Botanic Gardens at Kew, whose scientists initially didn't believe an amateur scientist—a *female* amateur—would be capable of making a discovery. But when Beatrix germinated her spores again and again, the Kew scientists tried the experiment themselves.

With the help and encouragement of her uncle Sir Henry Enfield Roscoe, a knighted and renowned chemist, Beatrix wrote about germinating spores in a paper for the Linnean Society, a group of London's foremost experts in natural history. Only men could participate in the society. It was Kew scientist George Massee who agreed in 1897 to submit the paper on Beatrix's behalf. The paper, entitled "On the Germination of the Spores of *Agaricineae*" (a suborder of gilled mushrooms), was not approved for publication, and Beatrix withdrew it from consideration. She wrote to Charles McIntosh that Linnean scientists said her paper needed more work before it could be printed.

The paper was never printed, and it was lost to history. Experts can only guess about whether she made a true discovery, because Beatrix's journal only hints at the focus of her work. The journal ended in 1897 shortly after she made contact with the Linnean Society. But she was later shown to be among the first British people to germinate spores from the group of fungi she worked with, basidiomycetes (pronounced *buh-SID-ee-oh-MY-seets*), which includes most mushrooms and toadstools. A century after she submitted her paper, the Linnean Society apologized for how it treated Beatrix and other women.

Beatrix juggled her passions for art and nature. The day after she found a rare fungus, she wrote the first draft of her most famous story in the form of a picture letter. Five-year-old Noel Moore, the son of her friend, was sick, so she wrote him a story about her bunny Peter Piper. She must have been thinking of fungi and her friend Charles McIntosh, because the Mr. McGregor character looked quite like him. Beatrix didn't pursue publication of *The Tale of Peter Rabbit* for another eight years. In the meantime, she grew more passionate about fungi.

During the decade Beatrix studied fungi, she wrote several other illustrated letters to children in addition to the one she had written to Noel. Noel's mother encouraged Beatrix to write books about her characters. In 1901 Beatrix made 250 copies of *The Tale of Peter Rabbit*. This attracted the publisher Frederick Warne & Co., which released her story widely the following year.

Beatrix went on to create dozens of books for children, including some published after her death in 1943. If you look closely, you'll find fungi in *The Tale of Squirrel Nutkin* (1903), *The Tale of Johnny Town-Mouse* (1918), and *The Fairy Caravan* (1929).

TIMELINE

1866   JULY 28: Helen Beatrix Potter is born in Kensington, a borough of London, England.

1871   On vacation in Scotland, four-year-old Beatrix first encounters Charles McIntosh, a postman and naturalist.

1887   Beatrix produces her first known drawing of a fungus.

1888–1898   Beatrix delves into mycology, the study of fungi.

1891   After selling drawings of rabbits wearing coats to one publisher, Beatrix submits sketches to the British publisher Frederick Warne & Co., which rejects them.

1892   Beatrix begins to exchange notes and drawings of fungi with Charles McIntosh, now retired from postal work.

1893   SEPT. 3: Beatrix discovers a fungus known as "Old Man of the Woods," a rarity in Scotland.

1893   SEPT. 4: Beatrix writes a picture letter to Noel Moore, her former tutor's five-year-old son, about her bunny Peter Piper.

1893   SEPT. 5: Beatrix writes a picture letter to Noel's four-year-old brother, Eric, about Mr. Jeremy Fisher the frog.

1897   George Massee, a published scientist, presents Beatrix's scientific paper to the Linnean Society of London. Women were not allowed at meetings. She eventually withdraws the paper from consideration because Society members say it needs more work.

1901   Beatrix self-publishes her rabbit story under the name "H. B. Potter."

1902   Frederick Warne & Co. reissues her first children's book, *The Tale of Peter Rabbit*. The first run of 8,000 copies sells out quickly.

1906   Frederick Warne publishes *The Tale of Mr. Jeremy Fisher*.

1913   Beatrix, age 47, marries William Heelis.

1943   DEC. 22: Beatrix dies of bronchitis and heart disease at age 77.

1967   Fifty-nine of Beatrix's fungi drawings appear in W. P. K. Findlay's book, *Wayside & Woodland Fungi*.

1997   The Linnean Society apologizes for treatment of Beatrix and other women.

Acknowledgments

I am grateful to Libby Joy of The Beatrix Potter Society, who made incisive suggestions that strengthened this manuscript, and to Nicholas P. Money, a mycologist, science writer, and professor at Miami University in Ohio, who vetted the science. That said, any errors are mine.

BIBLIOGRAPHY

Lear, Linda. *Beatrix Potter: A Life in Nature*. New York: St. Martin's, 2007.

Linder, Leslie. *The Journal of Beatrix Potter: 1881–1897*. 2nd ed. London: Frederick Warne, 1989.

McDowell, Marta. *Beatrix Potter's Gardening Life: The Plants and Places That Inspired the Classic Children's Tales*. Portland, OR: Timber Press, 2013.

Money, Nicholas P. *Fungi: A Very Short Introduction*. Oxford: Oxford University Press, 2016.

Moore, Anne Carroll. *The Art of Beatrix Potter*. London: Frederick Warne, 1955.

Potter, Beatrix. *Beatrix Potter: Letters to Children*. New York: Harvard College Library Department of Printing and Graphic Arts and Walker and Company, 1966.

Taylor, Judy. *Beatrix Potter: Artist, Storyteller and Countrywoman*. Rev. ed. London: Frederick Warne, 1996.

Taylor, Judy. *Beatrix Potter's Letters*. London: Frederick Warne, 1989.

SOURCE NOTES

Beatrix recorded her journal in a code she invented. This book quotes the English translation.

"to copy any beautiful object…": Linder, *The Journal of Beatrix Potter: 1881–1897*, 109.

"Joy of joys…": Linder, 337.

"Tiny fungus people singing…": Linder, 435.

"Curiously strong & pleasant": Taylor, *Beatrix Potter's Letters*, 19.

"They say it requires more work…": Taylor, 41.

FURTHER READING

Hopkinson, Deborah, illus by Charlotte Voake. *Beatrix Potter & the Unfortunate Tale of a Borrowed Guinea Pig*. New York: Schwartz & Wade, 2016.

Marshall, Linda Elovitz, illus by Ilaria Urbinati. *Saving the Countryside: The Story of Beatrix Potter and Peter Rabbit*. New York: Little Bee, 2020.

McPhail, David. *Beatrix Potter and Her Paint Box*. New York: Henry Holt, 2015.

Wallner, Alexandra. *Beatrix Potter*. New York: Holiday House, 1995.